TABLE OF CONTENTS

THE COMPETITORS

Some animals may look cute and furry. But they are actually **fierce** fighters! American badgers are tough animals. With their sharp teeth and claws, they are ready for any fight.

Bobcats are **solitary** and **territorial**. They mark and guard their territories to keep others away. Who would win if these two battled?

American badgers are **mammals**. They have yellowish gray or red fur on their bodies. Their faces are white with black stripes. They have short legs and flat bodies.

American badgers can be found across western North America, from Canada to Mexico. They make their homes in underground **burrows**. These badgers are **carnivores**. They hunt for **rodents**, small birds, and insects.

LEFTOVERS

American badgers sometimes store their food to eat later. One was seen burying an entire calf!

AMERICAN BADGER PROFILE

```
0       1 FOOT    2 FEET    3 FEET
```

LENGTH
UP TO 2.8 FEET
(0.9 METERS)

WEIGHT
UP TO 26 POUNDS
(12 KILOGRAMS)

HABITATS

GRASSLANDS

DESERTS

MARSHES

AMERICAN BADGER RANGE

■ RANGE

BOBCAT PROFILE

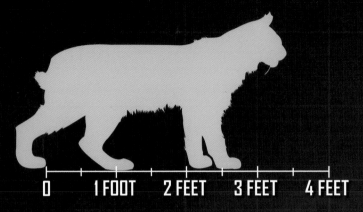

0   1 FOOT   2 FEET   3 FEET   4 FEET

LENGTH
3.4 FEET
(1 METER)

WEIGHT
UP TO 30 POUNDS
(14 KILOGRAMS)

HABITATS

FORESTS

SWAMPS

DESERTS

MOUNTAINS

BOBCAT RANGE

RANGE

Bobcats are sneaky mammals. They have reddish brown or tan fur with dark spots or stripes. Their bellies are white. Their short tails have black tips.

Bobcats make their homes in many **habitats** across North America. They mark their territories with scents and claw marks on trees. Bobcats often hunt small rodents. But they can also take down larger **prey** such as deer.

SECRET WEAPONS

BADGER CLAW

UP TO 1.75 INCHES
(4.4 CENTIMETERS)

Badgers' front paws have long, sharp claws. They can be up to 1.75 inches (4.4 centimeters) long! They use their claws to dig out prey. Badgers also slash at **predators** to **defend** themselves.

Bobcats' fur acts as **camouflage**. It allows them to sneak up on prey. Their fur may change colors with the seasons. This helps bobcats blend in with their **environments**.

Badgers have loose skin. It helps them make tight turns underground. It also helps badgers escape predators. Their loose skin makes it harder for enemies to hold on.

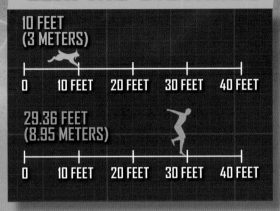

BOBCAT LEAPING DISTANCE

**10 FEET
(3 METERS)**

| 0 | 10 FEET | 20 FEET | 30 FEET | 40 FEET |

**29.36 FEET
(8.95 METERS)**

| 0 | 10 FEET | 20 FEET | 30 FEET | 40 FEET |

Bobcats use their long legs to climb high and leap far. From high up, they can search for prey. Once they spot prey, bobcats use their legs to pounce!

SECRET WEAPONS

LONG, SHARP CLAWS

LOOSE SKIN

STRONG JAWS AND SHARP TEETH

Badgers have strong jaws and sharp teeth. Their teeth sink into prey as their jaws snap shut. They rip prey apart as they bite off pieces of meat to eat.

BOBCAT

CAMOUFLAGE

LONG LEGS

SHORT JAWS AND SHARP TEETH

Bobcats also use their sharp teeth to take down prey. Their short jaws can bite down hard. Their teeth and jaws allow bobcats to kill prey in one bite.

ATTACK MOVES

Badgers are quick to attack when they feel danger. They **snarl** at their enemies. If enemies do not back down, badgers attack with their claws and teeth.

Bobcats mostly hunt under the cover of night. It keeps them hidden as they sneak up on their prey. Once they are close enough, they attack!

TOP SPEED

Bobcats can run as fast as 30 miles (48 kilometers) per hour!

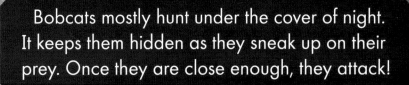

17

Badgers may give off a stinky smell to scare off predators.

Badgers use their loose skin to escape from enemies. They twist and spin when they are caught. Then, they turn around to bite their enemies.

Bobcats attack their prey from behind. They pounce on their prey's back and bite its neck. One bite is usually enough to finish the job.

READY, FIGHT!

A bobcat is on the hunt. It **stalks** a badger from the branches of a tree. Suddenly, the bobcat pounces! It grabs the badger with its claws.

The badger twists and turns before it sinks its teeth into the bobcat. But the bobcat holds on. It squeezes its jaws around the badger's neck. The badger just became the bobcat's meal!

GLOSSARY

burrows—tunnels or holes in the ground used as animal homes

camouflage—colors and patterns used to help an animal hide in its surroundings

carnivores—animals that eat only meat

defend—to protect

environments—the natural surroundings of areas

fierce—strong and intense

habitats—the homes or areas where animals prefer to live

mammals—warm-blooded animals that have backbones and feed their young milk

predators—animals that hunt other animals for food

prey—animals that are hunted by other animals for food

rodents—small animals that gnaw on their food; mice, rats, and squirrels are all rodents.

snarl—to growl while showing teeth

solitary—related to living alone

stalks—follows closely and quietly

territorial—ready to guard a home area

TO LEARN MORE

AT THE LIBRARY

Adamson, Thomas K. *Mountain Lion vs. Coyote*. Minneapolis, Minn.: Bellwether Media, 2021.

Downs, Kieran. *Wolverine vs. Honey Badger*. Minneapolis, Minn.: Bellwether Media, 2021.

Wilsdon, Christina. *Ultimate Predatorpedia: The Most Complete Predator Reference Ever*. Washington, D.C.: National Geographic Kids, 2018.

ON THE WEB

FACTSURFER

Factsurfer.com gives you a safe, fun way to find more information.

1. Go to www.factsurfer.com

2. Enter "badger vs. bobcat" into the search box and click 🔍.

3. Select your book cover to see a list of related content.

INDEX